SO-AVE-332

IMAGES
of America

ANGEL ISLAND

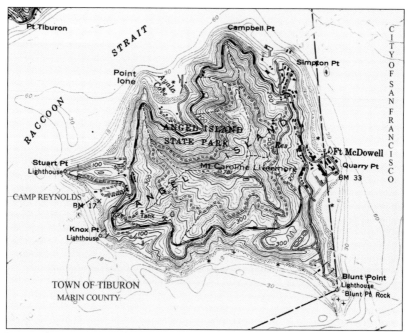

Pictured are a map and an aerial view of Angel Island. In 1946, the army lowered their flag on Angel Island and the State of California began planning for a state park.

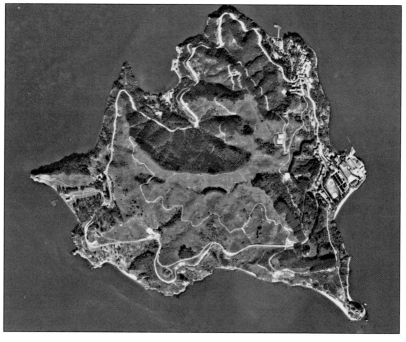

ON THE COVER: Angel Island, the largest island in San Francisco Bay, commands a dramatic location in southern Marin County.

IMAGES
of America

ANGEL ISLAND

Branwell Fanning and William Wong

ARCADIA
PUBLISHING

Copyright © 2006 by Branwell Fanning and William Wong
ISBN 978-0-7385-4719-0

Published by Arcadia Publishing
Charleston, South Carolina

Printed in the United States of America

Library of Congress Catalog Card Number: 2006935604

For all general information contact Arcadia Publishing at:
Telephone 843-853-2070
Fax 843-853-0044
E-mail sales@arcadiapublishing.com
For customer service and orders:
Toll-Free 1-888-313-2665

Visit us on the Internet at www.arcadiapublishing.com

CONTENTS

ACKNOWLEDGMENTS

This book could not have been written without the assistance of many generations of anonymous army historians who left a detailed record of life on the island. From the moment the first men of Company B, 3rd Artillery set up camps on a wild island outpost until their flag was lowered almost a century later, a steady stream of reports, photographs, and artifacts have made it possible for contemporary historians to gather the facts.

Another fantastic source of material were the private collections of Allyn Schaefer and Christopher Morrison. Schaefer has been enamored with Angel Island since childhood and now has the enviable position of boat operator on the State Parks Department Angel Island launch. Besides carrying park employees to and from Tiburon, Schaefer has been collecting photographs and postcards of the island for 30 years. Morrison operates a collectors shop called The Attic on Lower Ark Row in Tiburon. He too has been acquiring pictures and memorabilia of Angel Island since grammar school. Both of these gentlemen gave the authors complete access to their collections. Most of the aerial views are from the Brady Collection, now at the Marin History Museum.

Carolyn Fanning endlessly proofed the copy and produced a realistic sketch of the HMS *Raccoon* careened on the beach at Ayala Cove. Robin Adams and Casey Lee, employees of Angel Island State Park, gave guidance throughout the process of developing this fascinating story.

William Wong's expertise in immigration issues was invaluable to the Immigration Station chapter, of which he was the primary author. The remainder of the book was primarily written by Branwell Fanning. Also for Chapter Four, Dan Quan, an architect and exhibits designer and former president of the Angel Island Immigration Foundation, was especially helpful in sharing photographs from the foundation's archives and providing documents. Unless otherwise noted, all images are from the California Department of Parks and Recreation photographic archives. Others who offered help, advice, and counsel were Felicia Lowe, Daphne Kwok, Erika Gee, Connie Young Yu, Judy Yung, Christopher Chow, Phil Choy, Him Mark Lai, and Christine Schoefer.

Several books provided valuable historical background: *Miwoks to Missiles* by John Soennichsen, *At America's Gate* by Erika Lee, *Guarding the Golden Door* by Roger Daniels, and *Island: Poetry and History of Chinese Immigrants on Angel Island 1910–1940* by Him Mark Lai, Genny Lim, and Judy Yung.

INTRODUCTION

Ten thousand years ago, Angel Island, the largest island in San Francisco Bay, was part of the Tiburon Peninsula. A period of global warming thawed the glaciers covering much of North America; the oceans rose, and a mile wide gap separated Angel Island from the Marin County mainland.

For 200 years, every pirate, merchant ship, or explorer passing the fog-shrouded Golden Gate missed entering San Francisco Bay. The bay had been discovered by Europeans when, in 1774, an overland expedition led by Gaspar de Portola reached the southern end. In 1775, Lt. Juan Manuel de Ayala, captain of the Spanish ship *San Carlos*, did enter the bay and saw a giant land formation in the shape of a shark surrounded by water that was actually home to many sharks. He named the land Punta del Tiburon, or Shark Point. He found a sheltered cove on the large island just off the end of the peninsula and moored his ship.

Named Isla de Nuestra Senora de los Angeles by Lieutenant Ayala and Isla de la Santa Maria de los Angeles by Father Vincente (the chaplain on the *San Carlos*), it has been called Angel Island since the arrival of the Americanos. Ninety-eight percent of the island was incorporated as part of the town of Tiburon in 1964. Less than two percent of the 740-acre island is in the city and county of San Francisco.

Forty-six years after the visit of the *San Carlos*, Mexico won its freedom from Spain. Mexico seized the mission lands and granted property to settlers who were Catholic, could speak Spanish, agreed to live on the land, and demonstrated their loyalty to Mexico. From 1839 until 1860, the island was owned by a Mexican rancher, Don Antonio Maria Osio, who had received it as a grant from Mexico. Islands in the bay were not included in the Mexican land grants, so Angel Island became the property of the U.S. government. A ruling by the U.S. Supreme Court, after California was ceded to the United States and entered the Union, proclaimed the island government property and reserved it for defensive use.

The names of places on Angel Island were frequently changed. The cove known as Ayala Cove was called Hospital Cove for almost a century and Raccoon Cove, Glen Cove, and Morgan's Cove before that. Mount Caroline Livermore, the tallest peak on the island, was known as Mount Angel Island, or Mount Ida (although no one knows who Ida was), until it was named for Caroline S. Livermore, a leading environmentalist who worked to get the state to acquire the island for a park.

The army posts originally had individual names—Camp Reynolds, Fort McDowell, and Camp Simpton. In 1900, they were all combined to become Fort McDowell and renamed West Garrison, East Garrison, and North Garrison, respectively. North Garrison became home to the Angel Island Immigration Station. Its cove has been known as China Cove, then Winslow Cove in honor of the environmentalist who worked with Caroline Livermore, and back to China Cove again. Confusing? Of course. But we will try to keep it straight by using the names most commonly used today as much as possible. In this book, unless otherwise noted, Fort McDowell will refer only to the installation at East Garrison.

Any invading fleet entering San Francisco Bay would have as its goal the naval shipyard at Mare Island or the armory at Benicia, or so the Civil War military planners in Washington believed. The ships would have to pass close by Angel Island, so in 1863, defense works consisting of several gun batteries were constructed, and Camp Reynolds was established to house the soldiers manning these batteries. All shipping to ports in the North Bay or on the Sacramento River had to pass through narrow channels on either side of Angel Island. In the interest of safe passage, three lighthouses were built on the island with warning lights, foghorns, and bells operating when needed.

After the Spanish-American War, 126,000 soldiers returning from fighting in the Philippines had to be screened for tropical diseases at Angel Island hospitals. New recruits were trained and were issued travel orders at Fort McDowell. During and after World War I, Fort McDowell was handling 40,000 men per year, more than any post in the country.

The fear that a disease such as smallpox could be introduced into San Francisco by a ship coming from Asia required that the Public Health Service screen all passengers. After 1891, passengers entering San Francisco Bay and their luggage were off-loaded and transferred to a quarantine station installed on Angel Island. Passengers were checked for disease while luggage and cargo were fumigated. They had to stay in barracks until the entire ship had been cleared. This could take a month or more.

Congress passed the Chinese Exclusion Act in 1882, and for several decades the U.S. government enforced that law at a facility on the San Francisco wharf. That facility proved inadequate, and in 1910, authorities chose Angel Island as a new immigration station.

Thus, Angel Island played an important role in a significant change in official U.S. immigration policies. Those policies were all but nonexistent before the Chinese Exclusion Act. Once that act became law, the federal government began aggressive regulation of who entered the United States, first in San Francisco, then on Angel Island. This became a national model for how immigration policies were and continue to be implemented.

It is estimated that one million immigrants traversing the Pacific Ocean—the majority from China, Japan, and other Asian nations—were processed at the Angel Island Immigration Station. The total includes those coming to the United States and those leaving. For that reason, Angel Island has been called the "Ellis Island of the West." That designation, however, is somewhat of a misnomer, as Ellis Island was more of a facility to accept immigrants, whereas Angel Island's main purpose was to stop Chinese immigrants deemed excludable ("laborers" broadly defined).

After a fire on August 11, 1940, destroyed the administration building of the Angel Island Immigration Station, the facility closed; however, surviving buildings are currently being restored as a museum and educational center.

During World War II, 300,000 men were sent to the Pacific theater out of Angel Island posts. A POW camp had been set up for German prisoners during the war. The few Japanese who surrendered were held there before being sent to camps in the Southwest. By the time captured Italian soldiers got to Angel Island, Italy had changed sides in the war, and they were no longer POWs. But they still could not get home, so they became members of Italian Service Units and worked in the kitchens, laundries, etc. on army posts and navy bases around the bay.

The last military service of Angel Island came during the cold war. In 1952, the top of the island was sliced off for a radar station to control Nike missiles housed in silos on the island. The Nike air defense system was part of a plan to shoot down Soviet bombers before they reached U.S. shores. Intercontinental ballistic missiles made the system obsolete, and the missiles were removed in 1962.

Angel Island is now one of the most popular destinations in the California State Parks system. Several hundred thousand visitors a year are drawn by its beauty and its proximity to San Francisco. The island's history covers a wide and sometimes confusing variety of subjects—all of which we will try to make some sense of in this book.

One

THE EARLY YEARS

Lieutenant Ayala and his crew were greeted by friendly members of the Coast Miwok tribe, known as the Hookooeko, who had been living here for many thousands of years. There was no evidence of any permanent habitation on the island, but huge shell mounds marked the places where they had camped for extended periods. Shellfish formed an important part of the Miwok diet, and the then unpolluted waters of the bay were rich in oysters. Deer and other small game were plentiful, as were acorns, the staple in the Miwok food supply. There were several permanent villages on the peninsula just across Raccoon Strait, which would have made access easy for the reed boats used by the Miwoks.

When Mexico became independent from Spain, the property of the Catholic missions was secularized. The 8,000-acre Rancho Corte Madera del Presidio, awarded to John Thomas Reed, a native of Ireland, excluded any islands. In 1839, Angel Island was granted to Antonio Maria Osio, a native of Baja California. The island had been plagued with gangs of smugglers, pirates, and renegades even before Osio took possession. After he installed 500 head of cattle, rustlers added to the troubles. Richardson Bay became the winter home of the North Pacific whaling fleets of several nations, and they, and any other vessel visiting the San Francisco Bay, used the island to replenish their supplies of wood and water.

Richard Henry Dana, in *Two Years before the Mast*, spent a cold and wet night in 1835 on Wood Island, today's Angel Island, loading a year's supply of firewood for his ship. The island "called by the Spaniards 'Isla de los Angelos' was covered with trees down to the water's edge," wrote Dana. When Dana returned as a tourist 24 years later, the island was "clean shorn of trees." Fast-growing eucalypti were planted to replace the native trees and have been a problem ever since.

Before the Civil War, dueling over almost any slight was still in fashion, and Angel Island was a favorite site, drawing participants and scores of supporters. Fortunately, most were poor shots and few were seriously injured. One famous duel on the island featured prominent political figures, and they were accurate enough to shoot each other, unfortunately. Only one died, however. Dueling was outlawed soon after.

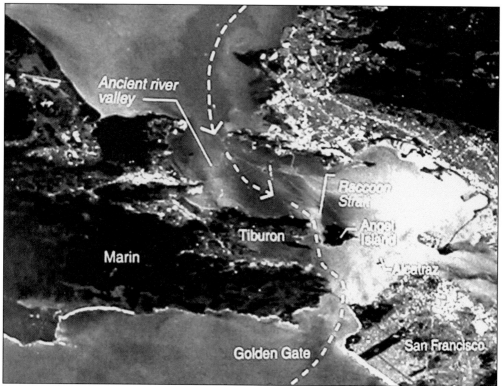

Many thousands of years ago, San Francisco Bay was a huge lake surrounded by many mountains. As the vast ice sheets melted and the oceans rose, the Golden Gate opened and the Sacramento River cut one mountain off the end of the Tiburon Peninsula. It became Angel Island, and the river's channel became Raccoon Strait. (NASA photograph; courtesy of the Angel Island Association.)

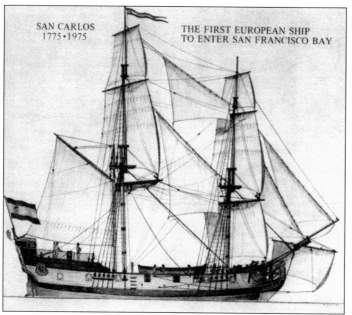

The Spanish ship *San Carlos*, built in 1767 in San Blass, Mexico, carried 30 officers and men although it was only 58 feet long with a beam of 17 feet. After creeping slowly into San Francisco Bay in August 1775, it found shelter in the lee of Angel Island in a spot now named Ayala Cove after its captain, Lt. Juan Ayala. Jose de Canizares, the sailing master on the *San Carlos*, spent several weeks in a small boat making the first maps of the Bay Area.

The HMS *Racoon* entered the bay in 1814, halfway through a disastrous voyage from England to the Pacific Northwest. Severely damaged on the reefs and shoals of the Columbia River, she was sinking and needed extensive repairs, but San Francisco was still a primitive outpost without shipyards or repair facilities. They managed to get the *Racoon* into the cove on Angel Island and careened the ship on the beach. The passage between the island and Point Tiburon retains the name, but with a different spelling— Raccoon Strait.

This drawing shows the island before the top 16 feet were removed for a radar station, part of the Nike system during the cold war. The top has recently been restored, making the island 797 feet high. This view from Sausalito shows ships in Whalers Cove—today's Richardson Bay—where the international whaling fleet would winter. The beginning of Camp Reynolds can be seen on the island.

Don Antonio Maria Osio (above left) was granted Angel Island by the Mexican authorities in 1839. He had been active in Alta California politics. Besides the 740 acres of Angel Island, Osio received grants of almost 50,000 acres in Point Reyes. After Mexico lost California, Osio took his family to live in Hawaii. He eventually returned to Baja California, where he died in 1878. For many years Osio raised a herd of 500 cattle on the island, but he lost the rights to his Angel Island properties in 1860 when the U.S. Supreme Court rejected his claim. By that time, most of his cattle had been stolen and squatters had moved onto the land. They had to be forcibly removed by the army. In granting Osio's original request for the island, the Mexican military commander General Vallejo had added a caveat protecting the government's right to fortify the island. In the 1860s, the U.S. agreed with Vallejo's assessment. It was not only fear of an attack by the South during the Civil War; the English fleet was also a concern. England might take advantage of the distraction of the Civil War to expand their holdings south of the Columbia River, and perhaps even occupy California. Below left, Osio's cattle were marked with this brand.

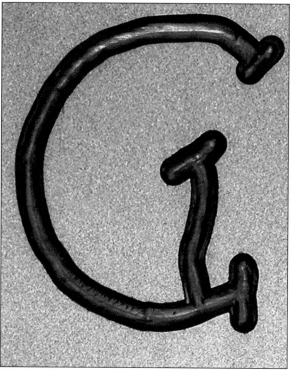

When the military took command of Angel Island, they also occupied Peninsula Island (which would later become Belvedere Island) with a small detachment of soldiers. The army claimed that it was not part of the Reed Ranch but was an island exempt from the original land grant. When in 1885 the Reed family was successful in establishing their claim to the island, the army moved out. This early map shows a ferry link from Angel Island to the tip of Belvedere Island.

Any attacking force that managed to get passed the fortresses on either side of the Golden Gate would now have to face gun batteries on Alcatraz and Angel Islands. Army engineers transformed Alcatraz from a barren rock into a fortress with 100 guns, using rock quarried on Angel Island. It was impossible to grow anything on Alcatraz, so gardens were planted on Angel Island to feed the troops.

Michael O'Donnell arrived in America in 1849, from Ireland. He soon found work as the "Keeper of the Quarry" on Angel Island. He and his wife, Julia, had eight children, who were all born on the island. Daughter Annie (left above) was born in 1864. Son Thomas (right), born in 1870, followed his father in managing the quarry and was still listed as a "stone cutter" in the 1920 census of Sausalito. The quarry operated until 1922 and was located at Fort McDowell.

James F. "Fred" Perle moved to Angel Island to act as a civilian blacksmith in 1886. He lived in this house overlooking a beach that for many years was known as "Perle's Beach." He also started a dairy farm. As the army bases expanded, Perle managed the pump house supplying water to the island. His son Fred Jr. carried on as rancher, farmer, and mechanic until he died in 1924.

Two

THE ARMY TAKES OVER

Eighty-three years after the army first set up camps on Angel Island, they lowered their flag and sailed away for good, or so they thought at the time. Angel Island had served the army well in the Civil War, the Indian Wars, the Spanish-American War, the Philippine Insurrection, and World Wars I and II. In 1946, the Pentagon thought that they no longer needed an outpost in San Francisco Bay.

The island was first occupied by the army when, in 1863, Company B, 3rd Artillery landed on the southwest corner of the island and began construction of Camp Reynolds and several gun batteries. By 1865, three batteries commanded Raccoon Strait and the Golden Gate. Two years later, the post was taken over by the infantry. During the 1870s, it served as a prison camp for Native Americans taken in the Arizona Campaign. In 1899, a quarantine station was established on the site known as Hospital Cove. The first troops returning from the Philippines were quarantined there until a detention station was established on the east side of the island. In 1900, the detention station was converted into a discharge depot, with permanent administration buildings and quarters. Fort McDowell became the headquarters for the 12th Infantry as well as the 9th. From the 1860s to the 1880s, both units fought in the Indian Wars throughout the western states.

Until 1941, Angel Island served as an overseas replacement and discharge depot. Troops bound to and from Hawaii and the Philippines were assigned transportation or discharged. With the outbreak of World War II, Angel Island became part of the San Francisco Port of Embarkation and was used as a staging area for large numbers of troops. With demobilization of the army following the Japanese surrender, the need for this facility diminished, and in mid-1946, the army garrisons on Angel Island closed and were declared surplus. They then passed into the control of the War Assets Administration.

After the Civil War, the importance of the artillery installations faded quickly, so Camp Reynolds was expanded to house and train infantrymen from around the West. This 1870s photograph shows a long row of barracks in the foreground and a number of officers' homes opposite them. The cannon in the lower right are more ceremonial than useful.

By 1876, Camp Reynolds had facilities for 200 soldiers, complete with barracks for the enlisted personnel, homes for officers and their families, a bakery, blacksmith, laundry, shoemaker, and barber. There was a trading store and, as seen in this photograph, a chapel on the hill above Officers Row. Gravestones are beginning to appear in the white fenced cemetery higher up the hill. This was the final resting place for army personnel who died on Angel Island or Alcatraz and for members of their families.

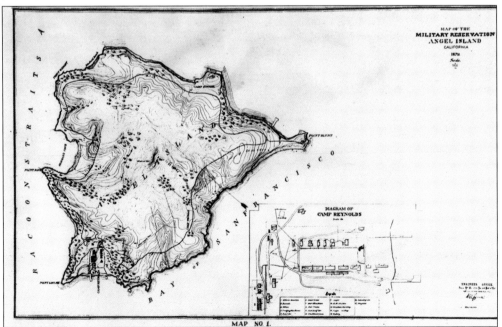

In 1879, the army drew this map of the Military Reservation Angel Island, including a detailed insert of Camp Reynolds. Note that the single "C" spelling of the strait between the island and the Tiburon Peninsula was still in use.

The parade ground had officers' housing smartly lined up on one side opposite these barracks for the men. It was likened to an ocean—an enlisted man did not cross the parade ground unless his presence was required.

At the head of Officers Row are two buildings known simply as Quarters No. 10 and No. 11. Built in 1867 on Yerba Buena Island, they were barged to Camp Reynolds in 1882. They have been used as officers' housing, quarters for non-commissioned officers, and lodging for a schoolteacher. Quarters No. 10 has been completely restored and is open to the public when docents are available.

Coast artillery batteries were first built at Point Stuart and Point Knox. Guns were also placed at Point Blunt but proved too difficult to service and were removed after rains washed out the installation. An 1886 report questioning the defenses of San Francisco Bay prompted the addition of batteries Ledyard, Wallace, and Drew on Angel Island. Five years later, the guns were obsolete and removed. Three 32-pound, smooth-bore cannon were mounted at Point Stuart. Seven 32-pound cannon, one eight-inch, and two 10-inch Rodmans were mounted at Point Knox.

A new casting process developed by Thomas Jackson Rodman, a West Point graduate, allowed the manufacture of mammoth guns for coastal defense. No ship, even the new ironclads, could stand up against a Rodman fired at close range. Eight- and 10-inch Rodmans were mounted on Angel Island. They were the last in a long line of smooth-bore, muzzle-loading cannon.

The three new batteries—Drew, Ledyard, and Wallace—and the rebuilt Battery Knox were armed with modern eight-inch, breach-loading steel rifles and similar guns by 1902. Although considered obsolete in the next decade, most of the guns were not removed until after World War I. During World War II, the sites for these three new coastal defense batteries were used to mount 90-mm antiaircraft guns.

The new batteries were protected by massive concrete bunkers. This bunker at Battery Drew is still open to the public.

The proximity to a popular city such as San Francisco and the ideal climate of Marin County made Angel Island duty far from a hardship posting. This officer and his ladies use the guns as their picnic ground. (Not exactly regulation, but the guns were probably obsolete anyway.)

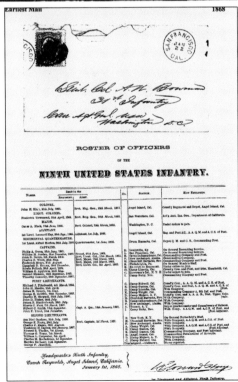

Angel Island did not get its own post office until January 1875, so this 1868 letter, sending a list of officers stationed on the island to headquarters in Washington, D.C., was postmarked from San Francisco. It is the earliest recorded piece of mail associated with Angel Island.

These Civil War–era troopers were ready to take on all comers. Recruits from all over the West were sent to Angel Island for initial training. They learned army customs and regulations and the basics of drilling. Combat training consisted of being told to "watch the man on either side of you and watch your sergeant!"

At the conclusion of the Civil War, the nation's attention turned to the West. The transcontinental railroad was completed, and the land was available for settlers. The infantry took over the coast artillery positions on Angel Island, turning them into a camp for recruit training and mobilization. Troops based here were engaged in campaigns against the Apache, Sioux, Modoc, and other tribes throughout the western United States. (Courtesy of the Bancroft Library.)

This beautiful little chapel was built in 1876, complete with stained-glass windows. It was named St. Marie, although who decided that is not known. It was also used as a schoolhouse for the 20 to 30 school-age children usually on the island. The chapel is still standing but in need of refurbishing.

Officers and enlisted men who were permanently stationed on Angel Island were permitted to have their families with them. The children had regular classes in the chapel and other buildings on the island. High school students rode an army ferry to Tiburon and attended Tamalpais High School. Note the size of the cannonballs in this photograph.

The Bake House is another early Camp Reynolds building that has been restored and is open to the public when docents are available. Next-door to Quarters No. 10, it was used to bake the bread, pies, and biscuits for the mess hall. Also nearby, and undergoing renovation, is the Mule Barn. The heavy work on Angel Island was done, as throughout history, by the faithful army mule.

The oven in the Bake House was not very elaborate, but in the practiced hands of army bakers it supplied the troopers with bread, biscuits, and a few extras. This simple oven could turn out 2,400 rations of bread per day. (A ration was enough bread to feed one man three meals each day.)

The uniforms would indicate that these troopers from Battery B were standing for morning inspection at Camp Reynolds sometime in the mid-1890s.

One private found the girl of his dreams on an outing in San Francisco. To avoid problems with young men away from the farms for the first time, attempts were made to keep them on the island as much as possible. Banks, railroad ticket offices, and recreation centers were provided on the post.

Even before the advent of germ theory in 1870, army doctors understood that separating sick patients from healthy troops cut down on the spread of disease; so hospitals were built away from the camps, usually downwind. In 1864, a small hospital was built at the cove, some distance from Camp Reynolds. It was only used until 1869 when a hospital was built closer to the camp. It was replaced in 1904 by this hospital, which can still be seen from the Tiburon waterfront. The journey to the hospital was a difficult one for a sick or injured trooper.

The waterfront at Camp Reynolds was a busy place. Most supplies for the island came across this wharf built in 1864. Warehouses and camp administration buildings were nearby. Most of these buildings are gone except for the brick warehouse built in 1909, which is now used by youth organizations for overnight stays.

This pier at the foot of the parade ground at Camp Reynolds was the main gateway for supplies, equipment, and men for the post. Regular service by government steamer to San Francisco was available for all residents, military and civilian. Because the roads were in such poor condition, communication between the various posts on the island was by ship. Pilings remaining after the piers were removed mark the location of the waterfront at Camp Reynolds.

Perhaps a dozen or more small ships provided the necessary communication and supply service for the various activities on Angel Island. The first were sailing vessels subject to the vagaries of wind and tide, but with the arrival of the steamer *General McPherson* in 1867, regular schedules could be maintained. These small ships also carried drinking water in tanks to pump ashore and fill the storage tanks on the island. The quarantine and immigration stations had their own fleet of service boats.

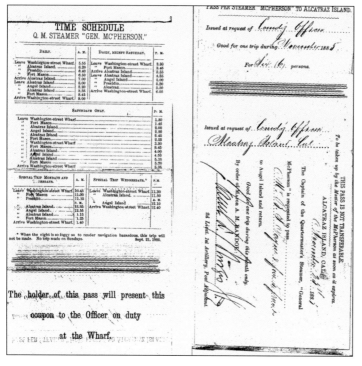

According to this 1885 schedule, the quartermaster steamer *General McPherson* traveled between downtown San Francisco, Fort Mason, the Presidio, Alcatraz, and Angel Island twice a day and was used by the quarantine and immigration stations when needed. It took 20 minutes to travel between Camp Reynolds and the Washington Street Wharf in San Francisco if traveling in a direct route. Another steamer, the *Frank Coxe*, is estimated to have carried six million passengers before being retired.

28

The first troops arriving home from the Philippines during the Spanish-American War were held at the quarantine station until they were cleared by health authorities, but that soon became overcrowded, so the army established this detention camp near Quarry Point. By 1901, the tide of veterans returning from the Far East grew even larger, and the army moved the detention camp to Point Simpton and converted this to a camp for troops waiting for discharge or reassignment. By 1907, 126,000 men had passed through the discharge camp on Angel Island.

Some of the earliest groups to pass though the detention camp were U.S. Army personnel returning from the Philippines. It was feared that they may have contracted various tropical diseases during the jungle warfare. The army soon built a discharge center elsewhere on the island.

Camp Reynolds was filled to overflowing at the time the U.S. entered World War I. For extra housing, "Sibley tents" were set up on the parade grounds. The main embarkation ports for Europe were on the East Coast, but Angel Island was the training ground for thousands of troops destined for the Pacific Islands and Panama. New recruits and others awaiting assignment to regiments in other areas had to remain on Angel Island until a group large enough to travel was assembled, which often could take months.

Quarry Point was named for a large block of limestone on the end of a peninsula on the east side of Angel Island. This rock was quarried to construct the forts on Alcatraz, used as breakwaters at the Mare Island Naval Base, and even in the construction of several downtown San Francisco office buildings. The large rock outcropping in this 1910-era photograph was completely quarried away when the army stopped quarry operations in 1922. It is still visible in the image at the top of page 31.

By 1909, the army had made the decision to make Angel Island the main base on the West Coast for recruit training and for discharge and transfers of troops. Fort McDowell became the center of a furious construction project, which saw the erection of the 1,000-man recruit barrack, mess halls, another hospital, parade ground, guardhouse, officers' homes, Post Exchange, and all the other facilities of an army post. "Temporary" wooden barracks were added during World War I.

The key building in the new Fort McDowell construction was the recruit barrack. It could house 686 men at the army's standard of 60 square feet per man. By double bunking, 1,000 men could be housed, giving it the unofficial name of the "Thousand Man Barracks." At the peak of World War II, Angel Island became the main staging base for troops heading to the Pacific. More than 300,000 men passed through during the war.

The new Fort McDowell would not be a repeat of the wood construction of Camp Reynolds but concrete buildings with tile roofs. Military prisoners from Alcatraz handled much of the construction using a new "tilt-up" method, and most interior walls were concrete blocks covered with several coats of plaster. In spite of age and considerable vandalism, this form of construction has held up well in this climate.

The last of the army hospitals built on Angel Island was at Fort McDowell. It was completed in 1912 in a central location at the fort. The new post hospital soon had an annex at the rear for long-term care patients. Average capacity, with the annex, was 106 beds, with room to expand to 209 beds when needed. The hospital closed when the army abandoned Angel Island in 1946. It reopened as a barrack to house the 100 troopers manning the Nike missile base just down the road.

As World War I approached, Fort McDowell soon began overflowing with new recruits, and out came the Sibley tents again. Each could hold six men and had two stoves—one for heating and one for cooking food. The parade ground and recreation fields were pressed into service for additional housing.

Temporary barracks were squeezed into every spare bit of space, and it was crowded. When not in training, the troopers could just hang out on the streets almost as if they were back home. These temporary barracks from World War I were still in use at the end of World War II.

Recruit training begins with learning the techniques of drilling, so the Fort McDowell parade grounds got a good workout as troops prepared to join regiments in the field.

New recruits marched everywhere. It would be a while before they filled out their new uniforms.

Hundreds of recruits poured into Fort McDowell as war in Europe looked inevitable. After the United States formally entered the war, the army population jumped to over 3,000, often with more than 4,000 passing through here each month.

The Regimental Band led the changing of the guard ceremony each morning. Members of army bands were not regular soldiers but recruited directly for the band. The 8th Infantry Band on Angel Island was almost entirely Italian, recruited on arrival from Europe. Even though some band members were the best shots in the regiment, they usually served as stretcher bearers if the regiment went into combat.

The Regimental Band sounds retreat, the army ceremony of retiring the colors each evening. Not all army posts had bands, but because Angel Island was a regimental headquarters, they had one. The band lived in quarters separate from the troops and even ate from their own kitchen. One bandmaster at Camp Reynolds did not approve of his quarters, demanded an ocean view, and got it. In peacetime, there was great competition among regiments for the best band.

Most army troop ships were too large to dock at Angel Island, so they berthed at Fort Mason in San Francisco. The "Angel Island Navy" of small steamers transported the troops destined for overseas duty to the embarkation piers and picked up the returning veterans. This continued until the end of World War II.

The Post Exchange at Fort McDowell was a popular place with troops stationed on an island without regular access to mainland shopping. It was a "one stop" shopping center for clothing, toiletries, and other supplies. It also had a restaurant, soda fountain, barbershop, and taproom (with beer on tap). Across Perimeter Road was a bowling alley and the paymaster's office.

The Fort McDowell Post Exchange had a full soda fountain, just like in San Francisco. Sandwiches, malts, and desserts were featured for hungry soldiers to enjoy in their free time.

A more formal event at the Officer's Club might bring out the regimental silver and embroidered napkins.

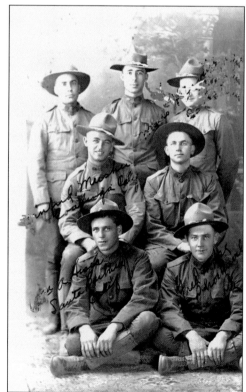

These World War I "doughboys" posed for a photograph to send to their families back home. Recruits made friends quickly on arrival at Fort McDowell.

Sporting a wide variety of hairstyles, these returning veterans wait with their buddies for their discharge so they could head for home with mustering-out pay (bonuses, travel pay, etc.) in their pockets.

Once the construction at Fort McDowell was complete, the administration headquarters was moved over from Camp Reynolds. This building was constructed along Officers Row as offices for headquarters staff.

Fort McDowell was the largest post on Angel Island, and its commanding officer (CO) was also the CO for all the army posts. A new home was built for him in the center of Officers Row. Because these houses were well built, a few survived, and employees of the California State Parks Department and their families reside in some of them today.

Like Camp Reynolds before it, Fort McDowell has a post chapel. It has been well maintained throughout the changes in management of Angel Island and is still used for weddings and other services.

San Francisco had many attractions that could have provided recreation for the troops, but because the army was building up fighting units, visits to these attractions were discouraged. Other recreation was limited because of the island's location. The beaches were available for those who liked cold water, and there were baseball diamonds for games. One of most popular spots was the army's YMCA right on the dock at Fort McDowell.

These World War II GIs were probably waiting for transportation to San Francisco to go out on pass. Being isolated on an island, even in San Francisco Bay, would not have a lot of appeal to young men, many away from home for the first time. Government steamers also were used to connect with troop transports at Fort Mason. The next stop would then be some South Pacific islands.

The Guard House, one of the buildings still standing and in good repair, is slated to be the Visitor Center at Fort McDowell. In the 1920s, the military prison on Alcatraz Island was closed, and the Angel Island Guard House became the primary lockup for less serious offences. The worst of the bad military prisoners went to Fort Leavenworth in Kansas.

The main mess hall could seat 1,400 at one time, and at the peak during World War II, the army was serving three groups at each meal, which meant serving 12,600 meals per day. Yet the food was considered pretty good for army chow, and they had some of the longest chow lines in the U.S. military. There were two floors in the mess hall. The upper floor was used to show movies, hold dances, and process troops being discharged when the fighting ended.

The main kitchen in the mess hall is where army cooks worked miracles getting everyone fed. There was no problem during the peacetime training of recruits, but when war came and the Angel Island population exploded, planning and organization was paramount. This was an island, after all. Everything had to be imported from the mainland.

These army cooks were augmented by members of an Italian Service Unit. Italy had surrendered in September 1943 with thousands of POWs in the United States. Like the German civilian seaman held for 14 months on Angel Island, they could not go home. They were formed into units who worked on military bases all over the Bay Area and were repatriated at the end of hostilities.

The main mess hall looks peaceful now, but when 200 tables were filled with hungry soldiers it was anything but quiet. In one memorable month in 1945, a total of 310,323 meals were served with little loss in quality, for which Angel Island was known. "Kitchen Police" duty was another thing. With that much activity, the KP worked from dawn to dusk and far into the night. And it was hard work.

When World War II ended in the Pacific, the goal was to get as many "home by Christmas" as possible. The "Magic Carpet" of transport ships, aircraft carriers, and anything else that would float brought up to 20,000 men into San Francisco Bay each day. The rail system was overwhelmed. Angel Island had every bed filled. During the war, about 50 buildings were erected next to the immigration station, and they were put into service along with immigration, the quarantine station, and Camp Reynolds.

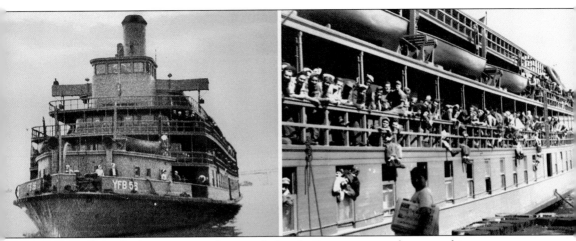

When the flow of military personnel reversed after the Japanese surrender, troop ships, passenger liners, and aircraft carriers arrived in San Francisco Bay loaded with a mixture of soldiers, sailors, and marines headed for home or individual service discharge centers. Even the old Sacramento River steamer, the *Delta Queen*, was pressed into service to help sort them out.

AUTHOR'S NOTE: As a young sailor, I served on the USS *Delta Queen, YFB-56* during Operation "Magic Carpet." We could carry up to 3,200 passengers on short trips between Fort Mason, where most troop ships docked; Alameda Naval Air Station, where an aircraft carrier hanger deck might hold 5,000 passengers; Treasure Island, where sailors and marines were discharged; or Angel Island, to drop off homebound soldiers. The *Delta Queen*, which moved to the Mississippi River in 1948, is one of the few U.S. Navy ships of World War II still afloat. (Branwell Fanning.)

Even though World War II was over and the future of Angel Island was in doubt, it still had one more role to play. With the help of the Italian Service Unit, these 60-foot-high letters welcomed home the troops who had fought the war in the Pacific.

Three

THE QUARANTINE STATION

There was a constant fear in San Francisco that some exotic tropical disease would arrive on a ship from the Far East. Smallpox, cholera, and the plague were still prevalent in China, Hong Kong, and Southeast Asia. Angel Island's relative isolation made it a target of the Public Health Service in their search for a location to set up a quarantine facility. Over the strenuous objections of the army, construction was begun on the Angel Island Quarantine Station in 1890. The first ship to be diverted to the station was the SS *China* in April 1891, with two cases of smallpox among the steerage passengers.

Ships too large to dock at the quarantine station were met by a small steamer, and all passengers and baggage subject to inspection were transferred to Angel Island. Steerage passengers, mostly Chinese, were forced to strip and be scrubbed and disinfected before moving to dormitories. Their baggage was also fumigated before being returned. Any passengers with actual infectious diseases were transferred to separate quarters where they received medical attention. Those who died were cremated on the spot. Those who survived were returned to the barracks until the quarantine period was over or returned to their homeland. Quarantine usually lasted from 14 to 21 days, depending on the suspected disease.

In 1864, the army built a small hospital to serve Camp Reynolds in the cove where the *San Carlos* anchored and the *Racoon* was careened for repairs. The name Hospital Cove stuck for almost 100 years, even though the original hospital lasted only until 1869.

In 1891, the new quarantine station (above) opened. It grew to 44 buildings, including the reception center, several bathhouses, medical screening rooms, dormitories for steerage passengers, separate dining rooms for both Chinese and Japanese passengers, isolation dorms for infected passengers, and a crematorium. Medical staff had homes on the station, and guards were posted by the army to prevent the possible spread of infections to military personnel.

The navy hulk *Omaha* was moored in Hospital Cove to provide live steam for the fumigation process. The *Omaha* was a navy steam schooner that was retired from active duty with its boilers intact. It was able to provide dry steam for the fumigation of baggage and whole ships when infection was detected.

Live, superheated steam for the fumigation was provided by the boilers in the *Omaha*. A combination of steam, formaldehyde, and ammonia was used as a disinfectant in these 40-foot-long, 7-foot-wide steel tubes. On arrival at the quarantine station, all baggage was opened, inspected, and then placed on small carts, which ran on rails through the tubes. After the quarantine period was over, the baggage was again disinfected before the passenger was allowed ashore.

Here is the reception area in the 1890s. Small ferries would bring passengers from ships too large to dock at the quarantine station. The *Omaha* was tied up there until 1914 when new forms of fumigation were developed. The buildings to the right were for the few cabin passengers who might have been exposed during the crossing. The center buildings were the homes of the senior medical staff and are still used by park personnel.

In the early 1900s, the steam launch *Bacilles* made frequent trips to the San Francisco waterfront to pick up passengers arriving on large ships unable to dock at the station. (Courtesy of Angel Island State Parks.)

The U.S. Public Health Service steamer *Millen Griffith* brought the steerage passengers and their luggage to the quarantine station on arrival in the United States. Most were from China. When several ships arrived on the same day, the station could be overwhelmed by detainees. The nominal capacity was about 1,100 persons, but there were times when 2,500 had to be accommodated, with some sleeping on the floor.

On reaching the dock at the quarantine station, the passengers' luggage was opened and inspected. It was then passed through the disinfecting tubes. The passengers were scrubbed with carbolic soap and issued overalls to wear while their clothing was being disinfected. The barracks were fumigated with sulfur dioxide and flushed with saltwater every morning.

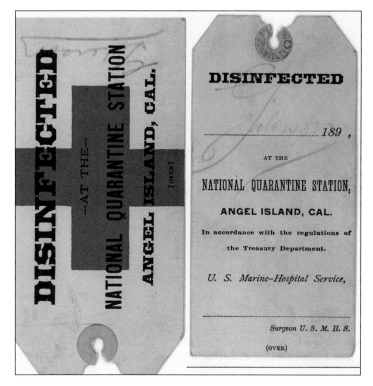

Passengers and luggage were "tagged" with this emblem issued by the surgeon from the U.S. Marin-Hospital Service at the National Quarantine Station, Angel Island. (Courtesy of Ken Harrison.)

The residences for the senior medical staff were built between 1890 and 1893, and the physicians assigned to the quarantine station lived in these quarters. Designated as senior surgeon and assistant surgeon, they worked under the surgeon general of the United States as head of the U.S. Public Health Service. Public health inspections improved overseas in the 1920s and 1930s, so the need for holding passengers in quarantine lessened. By 1940, the station was closed. Their homes are now used by park rangers and their families.

The last building constructed at the quarantine station was used for staff housing and administrative offices. Dating to 1935, it was still in good condition when most of the buildings were destroyed. The Visitor Center occupies the ground floor and is the first stop for those coming to Angel Island. The offices of the California State Parks Department and the Angel Island Association occupy the second floor. But first, it played host to some rather unusual visitors.

In the fall of 1939, the German ship SS *Columbus*, one of the largest and most luxurious passenger liners on the North Atlantic, sailed on a cruise to the Caribbean with 700 passengers and 700 crew. Then Hitler invaded Poland, and World War II began. The passengers were put ashore in Havana, and the captain was ordered to try to run the British blockade. Knowing that the chances of success were slim, the captain prepared his ship to be scuttled.

As the ship left the neutral waters of the eastern United States, British destroyers intercepted the *Columbus*. The captain ordered his crew into lifeboats and set fire to his ship. The entire crew was rescued by the U.S. Navy. As civilian sailors in a neutral port, they were entitled to be returned to their homeland. But how? The British were not going to allow 700 experienced seamen to return to become part of the German navy. An attempt to send them home via the Pacific on Japanese ships failed, leaving them stranded on Angel Island.

The crew of the *Columbus* spent about 14 months in what had been the quarantine station and the former immigration station. They were still employees of the North German Lloyd Company, who covered all the costs of their Angel Island stay, including food. The chefs on transatlantic liners were among the best in the world, and the detainees ate well during their confinement.

The crew did odd jobs around Angel Island, including fighting the fire at the immigration station administration building. For recreation they built a model, on display at the Visitor Center, of the *Pamir*, one of the last of the great sailing vessels carrying cargo between South America and Europe. Their status changed to that of enemy aliens after the United States entered the war. They were transferred to camps in the Southwest, finally getting back to Germany in 1946, seven years after sailing on a Caribbean cruise.

THE PIGTAIL HAS GOT TO GO.

Popular mass-market magazines like *Puck* and *Wasp* regularly featured drawings that fed the anti-Chinese sentiment prevalent in the nation in the mid- to late 1800s. These images helped shape political and public opinion, which became part of the Chinese Exclusion Act of 1882. The U.S. government established an immigration station on Angel Island to regulate the entry of Chinese and other Asian immigrants from 1910 to 1940. (Photograph by William Wong; Phil Choy collection.)

Four

THE IMMIGRATION STATION

The discovery of gold near Sacramento, California, in 1848 caught the attention of people around the world, including the Chinese of the Pearl River Delta in southeastern China. Chinese from this poor region, frequently ravaged by natural disasters, joined Europeans, Latin Americans, and Americans in the famous California gold rush of 1849. That was the beginning of the first significant Asian presence in the United States. In the Pearl River Delta region of China, California and the United States were called *gum saan*, literally "gold mountain."

Like other fortune seekers, the Chinese spread out throughout the Sacramento region and the California foothills. Unlike the others, the Chinese soon faced hostility and legalized discrimination. Many fled to new cities like San Francisco, Oakland, and Sacramento for refuge. There they found work as merchants, laborers, and farmers, among other trades.

As California grew, industrialists and other big-money interests sought out the Chinese as cheap labor. They were hired to build the western half of the transcontinental railroad. After it was built in the late 1860s, an economic downturn occurred. That volatile situation ignited an ugly political movement whose goal was the elimination of Chinese laborers, viewed by the white labor movement as cheap and competitive. The magazine cover on the facing page (page 56) was typical of the mass-media sentiment of the time.

The anti-Chinese fervor spread east to Washington, D.C., where Congress passed the Chinese Exclusion Act in 1882. The act barred the further legal entry of Chinese laborers, restricted Chinese immigration to a small group (merchants and students, primarily), and prohibited some American-born Chinese from becoming U.S. citizens.

From that point on, the U.S. government monitored and strictly regulated the entry of Chinese into America. First it did so from a San Francisco port facility. Then it built an immigration station on the north shore of Angel Island, which opened on January 21, 1910, and operated until August 11, 1940, when a fire burned the administration building.

Other immigrants (Japanese, Indians, Russians, other Europeans, and Africans) entering the United States via the Pacific Ocean were also processed at the Angel Island Immigration Station. But the Chinese, estimated at 175,000 in the 30-year life of the Angel Island Immigration Station, were specially targeted for lengthy and sometimes harsh interrogations because of the exclusion act.

Here is a panoramic view, looking north, of the immigration station in its earliest days. The dock and wharf are on the left, the administration building is in the left center, the heating plant is in the front foreground, the detention barracks are on the right, and the hospital is in the center background. The total contract to build these buildings was $129,773. The buildings were

This is a bird's-eye view of the immigration station looking south, around 1927. The administration building is in the foreground. Behind it are the detention barracks, with stairs leading to the dining facility. The hospital is on the hill to the left, and the row of cottages on the left is staff housing. Throughout the station's 30-year history, criticisms about the facility's construction, architecture, and operations came from immigrants and government officials.

completed in 1908, but the station didn't open until January 21, 1910. The U.S. government felt this was a better, more secure site than the San Francisco docks for a place to regulate immigration from Asia, especially China, since the Chinese Exclusion Act of 1882 barred the legal entry of Chinese laborers.

After immigrants put most of their belongings into a storage facility on the wharf, they were herded into the administration building for initial health inspections. Here the detention barracks are barely visible behind the administration building. The administration building housed the office of the U.S. commissioner of immigration and a few other staff members. For much of its existence, female immigrants lived on the second floor.

The detention barracks, with the staircase that led to the dining space, held at any one time 200 to 300 males and 30 to 50 females, segregated by race, ethnicity, and gender. Living conditions were crowded and uncomfortable. This photograph was taken around 1909, just before the formal opening of the immigration station in early 1910. Women detainees were eventually moved to the second floor of the administration building.

This is the main waiting room of the administration building, where newly arrived immigrants were initially processed. U.S. Public Health Service personnel examined them for possible communicable diseases before detainees were assigned a bunk in the detention barracks.

Cooks, mostly Chinese, commuted to Angel Island from San Francisco via ferry. The food, generally criticized throughout the station's 30 years, was different for Chinese and Asian detainees versus Europeans. Some Chinese kitchen staffers helped Chinese immigrants by picking up "coaching papers" at San Francisco Chinatown stores. The papers helped immigrants get through the interrogations, part of elaborate plans of immigrants to circumvent the Chinese Exclusion Act.

Barbed-wire fences reminded immigrants that their freedom was restricted. The immigration station was a low-security facility and did not have guard towers until the 1930s, when federal prisoners were also housed at the station. Guards were not armed. Nonetheless, Chinese immigrants, though technically not prisoners, felt as though they were being held in a prison-like setting. (Courtesy of the National Archives and Records Administration.)

This northward view shows San Francisco Bay in the background and a ferry launch. The hospital is on the right, and the administration building and the attached dining facility are on the left. While this view is gorgeous, detainees spent little time enjoying it. Males were generally confined to the barracks and got a little recreation-yard time. Females had a little more freedom to move about the grounds of the facility.

Joseph R. Silva was the station's head gardener for years. He took pride in making the grounds lush and beautiful. In fact, he became a reason why San Francisco's commissioner of immigration recommended to Washington, D.C., that certain station maintenance staff live in cottages on the grounds. Silva, his wife, and two children lived in one of the staff cottages.

This is the main barracks room without its rows of iron bunks. This room housed several hundred Chinese male detainees at a time and was often overcrowded. It was on the walls of this room that some detainees wrote or carved poems to express their frustration, anger, and wonderment at their incarcerated situation. This building is being restored as a museum as part of a private-public partnership.

This poem, carved into the wall of the men's barracks, is undated but was most likely after 1921, since this poem refers to a Mexican law excluding Chinese too. The last two stanzas say, "Don't say that everything within is Western styled. Even if it is built of jade, it has turned into a cage." In all, 135 poems were initially documented, with another 85 discovered in subsequent years. (Photograph by Chris Huie; Paul Chow collection.)

This photograph shows the mode of transportation for immigrants processed and/or detained at the Angel Island Immigration Station. In this case, these are immigrants leaving the island, cleared to enter the United States in San Francisco. The warehouse where most immigrant belongings were stored is on the left.

The steamer *Angel Island*, launched in 1911, became the main means of transportation for the immigration station. More than 16,000 passengers a month traveled on the *Angel Island*. Immigrants were segregated even during the relatively short transport to and from San Francisco—Europeans on the upper deck, Asians on the deck below.

The standard procedure by the U.S. immigration service at the time of the Angel Island Immigration Station was to have inspectors board ships carrying Chinese immigrants to check identification documents. That was the first step in processing Chinese immigrants as part of the enforcement of the Chinese Exclusion Act.

After the initial shipboard inspections, immigrants disembarked and, once their luggage was placed in the storage shack near the wharf, headed for the administration building for an initial medical examination by the U.S. Public Health Service. This is an early photograph of Chinese immigrants landing on Angel Island, around 1910, the year the immigration station opened. (Courtesy of the National Archives and Records Administration.)

This undated photograph of Chinese male detainees, both adults and children, shows them gathered somewhere on the grounds of the immigration station. By the look of some of their clothing, the time could have been sometime in the 1910s. (Paul Chow collection.)

This undated photograph, perhaps staged, shows Chinese women immigrants presumably registering in the office of the U.S. immigration commissioner in the administration building, with the help of a Chinese male interpreter. More routinely, immigrants registered in another part of the administration building, standing up at a podium.

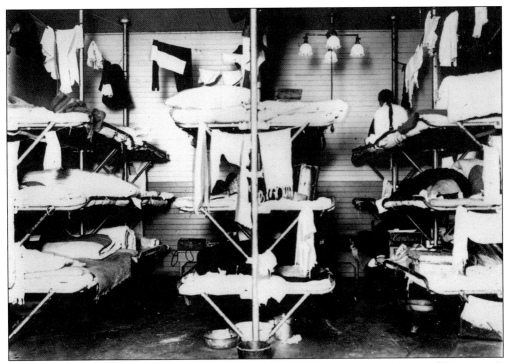

This is a rare photograph of the occupied bunks in the detention barracks, this one of the women's quarters. It shows the typical living conditions that Chinese immigrants endured. There were no chairs. Throughout the station's 30-year history, there were many complaints from immigrants (and some officials too) about the overcrowded, unsanitary conditions. (Courtesy of the California Historical Society; Paul Chow collection.)

The dining room—connected by a staircase to the detention barracks—was a crowded, noisy place. Immigrants complained constantly about the low quality of the food, prepared mostly by Chinese cooks but supervised by white officials. Detainees ate in segregated shifts and even had different menus. In 1919, a riot broke out in the dining room, necessitating federal troops to restore order. (Courtesy of the California Historical Society; Paul Chow collection.)

Only Chinese immigrants were subjected to sometimes lengthy, often inane, interrogations conducted by U.S. immigration inspectors, aided by interpreters. Their purpose was to determine the validity of an immigrant's application for legal entry into the United States. In large part, this process was a cat-and-mouse game, with U.S. inspectors hoping to catch immigrants in falsehoods about their identities and lives in China.

This is a typical "coaching" document—hidden in a banana—used by Chinese immigrants before they were interrogated. Coaching papers were a way to get around the Chinese Exclusion Act. Many Chinese male immigrants bought identities of false "paper sons" claimed by U.S. Chinese men visiting China. Coaching papers aligned the two separate identities. (Courtesy of the National Archives and Records Administration.)

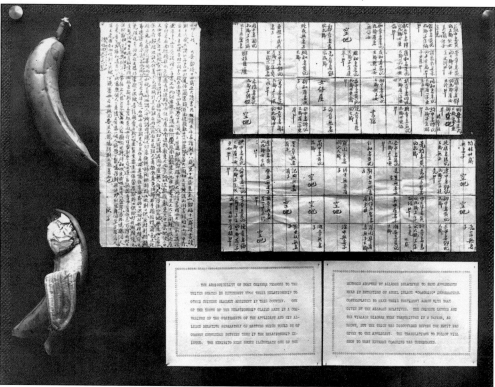

Immigrant children younger than 12 were kept with their mothers. It was rare for children of different races, ethnicities, and nationalities to mingle together, but in this case, a young white immigrant, possibly from Canada, stands with a Chinese male toddler in an undated photograph. Chinese children were part of families of merchants, a class of immigrants allowed to legally immigrate, but detained nonetheless to verify their true identities.

A Chinese woman oversees some Chinese children in this undated photograph. Even though women and children were in the numerical minority, they too were detained until immigration inspectors could clear them. Generally, Chinese women were discouraged from immigrating because men were thought to have a better chance to make a fortune in America and because of American suspicions that Chinese women were of low moral value or would need public assistance.

A young Chinese girl carries a baby, possibly her younger sibling, in this undated photograph. All children, except for infants, were interrogated. "It was just the way they confined you, like in a prison, that made us feel degraded," one detainee told the authors of *Island: Poetry and History of Chinese Immigrants on Angel Island 1910–1940*. He was 12 years old in 1933.

Two Asian girls, one in a traditional Japanese dress (left), the other in a traditional Chinese dress and head covering (right), pose together in this undated photograph. It is unlikely they were housed together with their female elders.

These six Chinese children are in traditional outfits and head coverings, indicating this photograph was mostly taken in the 1910s. They were probably children of merchants seeking legal entry into the United States.

In this undated photograph, a mixed group of women, predominantly Chinese, gather outside. Class considerations made entry to the U.S. difficult for some Chinese women. Merchants' wives and those traveling first class were considered more acceptable, whereas independent women were suspected of being immoral. Even so, merchant wives and children were questioned vigorously to prove their Chinese male sponsor was who he said he was and their relationship to him was legitimate.

Many Chinese male immigrants wanted to bring their wives and families, but various U.S. laws made that nearly impossible. One exception was the wife of a merchant. From 1910 to 1924, three of four Chinese female immigrants were "dependents," meaning the wife of a merchant, while the rest were single. The status of the three women in this undated photograph is unknown.

In a photograph taken perhaps in the 1910s, these Chinese women and children pose on a sloping pathway. The percentage of Chinese women coming to the United States increased steadily—from 0.7 percent of all Chinese entering in 1900 to 26 percent in 1930. Chinese women were relatively less scrutinized than Chinese men in the latter years of Angel Island because officials felt men lied more about their identities. (Paul Chow collection.)

Katherine Maurer (rear, right row) sits in this undated photograph with some Chinese women and children inside the detention barracks. Maurer was a dedicated Methodist deaconess who served at the immigration station from 1912 to 1940. Many Chinese women detainees, in later years, remembered the good work Maurer did.

Japanese "picture brides" lined up opposite their future husbands, ready to disembark at Angel Island. The picture brides were part of the wave of Japanese immigrating to the U.S., following the decline of Chinese immigration after the Chinese Exclusion Act. Because most Japanese immigrants were men and mixed marriages were outlawed, they sought Japanese wives through photographic communications. Japanese were not subjected to the same restrictions as Chinese, but starting in 1924, Japanese immigration became severely restricted.

A Japanese picture bride heads for the administration building toward an uncertain new life. This method of arranging a marriage had its downside. Sometimes the man sent a much younger (and thinner-appearing) photograph. When his bride saw him in person, she was shocked. Or the man may have fibbed, saying he was of higher economic status than he really was. A few brides changed their minds, asking to go home to Japan.

Japanese picture brides registered for legal entry into America at the immigration station. Picture brides were classified as "non-laborer," but some joined their husbands in the farm fields of California. This deception upset American labor organizations, which did not like the competition. This photograph was taken in 1916, according to the calendar on the wall.

Three Japanese picture brides pose on a hillside overlooking the San Francisco Bay. An exemption in the "gentlemen's agreement" between the United States and Japan allowed picture brides to join their future husbands in America. The busiest period for Japanese picture bride arrivals was approximately 1910 to 1920, when Japan stopped issuing visas to women for such a purpose. In all, an estimated 6,000 to 19,000 Japanese picture brides came through Angel Island.

Chinese were the most numerous Asian immigrants, followed by Japanese picture brides. Indians, however, also came through Angel Island. Here, in an undated photograph, are some Sikh men from the Punjab region of India, perhaps headed for the California farm fields to work as laborers during the 1930s. Asian farm workers—Chinese, Japanese, Filipinos, and Indians—were everywhere in the California agricultural fields in the late 19th and 20th centuries.

Largely known for processing Chinese and other Asian immigrants, the immigration station also dealt with people from other parts of the world. Here, in an undated photograph, are some Russian male immigrants. When they arrived is unknown, but some Russian Jewish men were on Angel Island by 1915, before the Bolshevik Revolution started. Generally, they were poorer than Russians, who fled after the revolution, arriving at Angel Island about 1921.

When these Russian women and children arrived at Angel Island is uncertain, but the California State Park Archives, from which this photograph was obtained, estimates it was 1917. "Russian refugees from Bolsheviks" was handwritten on the back of the archives print. Given that Russia is such a huge country, it is not surprising that some Russians, seeking better lives in America, would cross the Pacific Ocean rather than go through Europe.

The nationality of these European women and children is unknown; they could be Russians. They lived separately from Chinese and other Asian immigrants and ate at different times with different menus. They also were examined and scrutinized less stringently than Chinese immigrants were.

Three European immigrant women of unknown nationality get some fresh air in this undated photograph. The U.S. government did not keep regular statistics of immigrant nationalities other than Chinese, but immigrants from around the world and emigrants—those leaving the U.S.— went through Angel Island. Katherine Maurer, the Methodist deaconess who served at the immigration station for years, once called it "The Grand Hotel," referring to the diversity of people passing through.

An African mother and two children pose for this undated photograph. While African immigrants were not numerous, some were processed at Angel Island.

The great majority of Italian immigrants entered the United States through Ellis Island in New York in the late 19th and early 20th centuries, but some also came through Angel Island, such as the men and boys in this undated photograph.

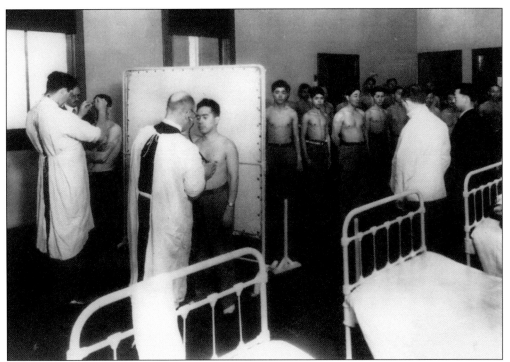

The U.S. Public Health Service examined Chinese immigrants, and American medical personnel operated on preconceived ideas that Chinese were more diseased than Europeans. For instance, they looked for certain parasitic diseases common among Chinese immigrants, hoping to use such discoveries to deport them. These diseases were treatable and did not pose a serious public-health threat, but Chinese found with such ailments were nonetheless detained or deported.

Chinese immigrant boys are examined for possible communicable diseases. This kind of examination of men and boys without shirts was shameful and embarrassing to many Chinese because they were not accustomed to being half naked in front of strangers.

In this 1934 photograph, immigration commissioner Edward Cahill, right, chats with some Chinese immigrant men and boys standing on the steps leading to a recreation yard. This was a rare moment of relaxation for male detainees, who spent most of their time in the barracks without much to do. Some expressed their anger and frustration by writing or carving poems into the wooden walls.

In this 1930s photograph, Chinese immigrant men relax in the recreation yard, which was behind and higher than the detention barracks. Note the guard tower on the right. Two guard towers were built on the grounds of the immigration station in the 1930s, and they were thought to be necessary to prevent escapes by federal prisoners—not immigrant detainees—held during that decade.

Playing volleyball was one of the few recreational activities allowed to the Chinese male detainees. From the look of some of their outfits, this photograph was probably taken in the 1910s. (Courtesy of Frances Maurer Schneider.)

The immigration station administration allowed Christmas parties to be held, planned, and carried out by Katherine Maurer, a Methodist deaconess, and other Christian missionaries who regularly visited the immigrant detainees.

In this photograph, probably taken in the 1910s, a Chinese missionary preaches to detainees. This activity was one way that detainees got fresh air and sunshine, but it is not known how many, if any, of the Chinese actually converted to Christianity. In U.S. Chinatowns, however, Christian churches have played—and continue to play—important roles in the lives of some Chinese Americans, both socially and spiritually.

In addition to listening to religious preachings, immigrants had other activities, such as lessons from Methodist deaconess Katherine Maurer (wearing a bonnet and dark suit on the right), who met regularly with female detainees to teach them English and the Bible. In this case, the women appear to be of different races, ethnicities, and nationalities even though they did not live together in the same barracks.

Chinese detainees called Methodist deaconess Katherine Maurer, pictured here with a group of them, "Kuan Ying," the Chinese goddess of mercy, for her good works over 28 of the 30 years of the immigration station's life. Among other things, she provided toiletries and clothing and even helped some detainees get jobs once they left Angel Island, in addition to English lessons and Bible studies.

Katherine Maurer also worked with non-Chinese, non-Asian immigrant detainees. In this undated photograph, she helps some European immigrant men, possibly Italian, work on a flag or some other craft activity.

Tye Leung, left, with an unidentified "matron," was the first Chinese woman hired, in 1910, to help supervise female detainees. Affiliated with Donaldina Cameron's Presbyterian Mission Home in San Francisco, she was an interpreter but also watched for prostitutes among them. That some Chinese women were prostitutes in the United States speaks to their oppressive status at the time. In 1912, Leung married a white immigration inspector. Because of prevailing racial-separatist attitudes, both resigned from their jobs. (Photograph by Frederick Schulze.)

U.S. immigration inspectors regularly examined the belongings of immigrants, looking for evidence that might disprove their claim of a right to gain legal entry into the United States. Inspectors assumed that Chinese immigrants lied about their identities and circumstances to circumvent the Chinese Exclusion Act. This photograph of an unidentified inspector and an immigrant was taken around 1916.

The immigration station had a good-sized staff, at least in the 1920s and 1930s. The Chinese pictured were interpreters, not inspectors, and white supervisors distrusted some of them. Corruption among some staff members, white and Chinese, was a problem. Some took payoffs to help smuggle out detainees or helped Chinese immigrants get "coaching papers" to smooth the latter's stringent interrogations. Some staff members found enforcing the Chinese Exclusion Act to be frustrating.

The staff of the immigration station's heating plant, or powerhouse, lived in cottages in the hills above the administration building.

Charles Thau, pictured here in this undated photograph with his son, was a maintenance worker who lived with his family in Cottage No. 9. Maintenance workers were among a small group of station employees who lived in the cottages on Angel Island designed by the famous architect Julia Morgan. A few staff members lived in the administration building, and others had to commute from San Francisco.

This unidentified staff family poses next to the storage shed on the wharf in this photograph taken most likely in the early 1910s. The heating plant is behind the two men, while the administration building is on the left.

While technically not part of the immigration station staff, Chinese missionaries, pictured here with Methodist deaconess Katherine Maurer (center), were part of Christian support groups that sought to make life more bearable for Chinese detainees.

The immigration station got international attention in 1939 when the U.S. government held deportation hearings, conducted by the dean of the Harvard Law School, for Harry Bridges, an Australian-born San Francisco labor leader. Bridges led an international longshoremen's strike along West Coast ports in 1934, and some political leaders accused Bridges of being a Communist and demanded his deportation. The government held the hearings on Angel Island to avoid mob violence in San Francisco. Bridges was eventually cleared of those charges and was not deported. He later became a U.S. citizen.

A fire, caused by a short circuit, broke out around midnight on August 11, 1940, in the administration building and burned most of the night. No detainees or staff were killed. Officials had already been planning to move the immigration station, and the fire coincidentally hastened its closure. The government set up a new immigration station in San Francisco, thus ending a troubled 30 years for the station on Angel Island.

Even though the 1940 fire did not destroy the detention barracks, detainees were first moved to another part of Angel Island and later to a San Francisco facility, pictured here. In 1943, Congress repealed the Chinese Exclusion Act, but legal immigration from China remained highly restricted until 1965 when Congress liberalized immigration laws by equalizing the worldwide annual quota. The 1965 changes profoundly altered the complexion of American society.

After the 1940 fire, what was left of the immigration station became a prisoner-of-war camp holding German and Italian soldiers, as well as interned seamen from the German luxury passenger ship *Columbus*. This German inscription is undated but may have been carved by a German POW during World War II onto the barracks wall of the immigration station. It means "shut the door" and is more of a command than a request. (Photograph by and courtesy of Dan Quan.)

In 1970, just before the immigration station buildings were to be torn down, state park ranger Alexander Weiss noticed some carvings on the barrack walls. He contacted Dr. George Araki of San Francisco State University, who concluded that the carvings—Chinese poems—had historical significance. This discovery launched the Asian American community's effort to save the barracks with their historically significant poems. (Photograph by and courtesy of Connie Young Yu.)

In 1971, the former immigration station site was the setting for a fire scene in the movie *The Candidate*, starring Robert Redford. The production company burned nine of the staff cottages. This incident did not play a significant role in the community effort to save the immigration station. That campaign started in earnest a few years later when the Angel Island Immigration Station Historical Advisory Committee formed. (Courtesy of the Angel Island State Park Slide Library.)

Paul Chow, a native San Franciscan, was a founder of the Angel Island Immigration Station Historical Advisory Committee in 1974. That committee later became the Angel Island Immigration Station Foundation, spearheaded by Chow, whose father had been detained on Angel Island. Chow, a civil engineer, was tireless in his crusade to preserve the immigration station before he passed away in 1998 at the age of 69. (Courtesy of Dorothea Char; Paul Chow collection.)

Christopher Chow, right, a founder of the Angel Island Immigration Station Historical Advisory Committee but unrelated to Paul Chow, conducts a tour in 1975. At that time, the committee was the only group authorized to lead such tours. In 1976, the committee persuaded the California legislature to appropriate $250,000 to restore and preserve the detention barracks as a state monument. (Photograph by Nancy Wong; Christopher Chow collection.)

A monument memorializing Chinese immigration through Angel Island was dedicated on April 28, 1979. The Chinese poem on the black granite monument reads, "Leaving their homes and villages, they crossed the ocean/Only to endure confinement in these barracks/Conquering frontiers and barriers/they pioneered/A new life by the Golden Gate." Ngoot P. Chin of San Francisco wrote the poem in a community competition sponsored by the *Chinese Times*. (Photograph by Kou-ping Yu; Connie Young Yu collection.)

Pictured with Lawrence Jue (left) and Paul Chow (right), San Francisco restaurateur Vic Bergeron (with microphone) donated the black granite monument marking the story of Chinese immigration through Angel Island. His popular Polynesian-style restaurant, Trader Vic's, employed many Chinese immigrant workers, whom he greatly appreciated. "Everything I am I owe to the Chinese," he once said. (Photograph by Kou-ping Yu; courtesy of Connie Young Yu.)

The California legislature commended the Angel Island Immigration Station Historical Advisory Committee for saving the immigration station and the poems in the detention barracks. Committee members attending a state capitol commendation event in 1981 are, from left to right, Jack Hesemeyer of the California Department of Parks and Recreation, Lawrence Jue, Paul Chow, state park ranger Alexander Weiss (who discovered the poems in 1970), Connie Young Yu, and Philip Choy. (Connie Young Yu collection.)

The detention barracks are being restored, including the poems carved into the walls. Ever since efforts began in the 1970s to save the station, the barracks have received many visitors, including thousands of school children. The Angel Island Association, working with the Angel Island Immigration Station Foundation (successor to the Angel Island Immigration Station Historical Advisory Committee) and the California Department of Parks and Recreation, conducts regular docent-led tours. (Photograph by Dan Quan.)

One of the most striking features of the saved detention barracks is the display of tiered bunks where Chinese and other immigrants used to sleep, rest, and pass the time. It is a reminder of the crowded conditions under which detainees lived for weeks and even months while their applications for admission to the United States were scrutinized, examined, and investigated. (Photograph by Dan Quan.)

The immigration station became a National Historic Landmark in 1997. The prestigious designation forges a partnership between the National Parks Service, the California Department of Parks and Recreation, and the Angel Island Immigration Station Foundation. At a 1998 celebration, John Knott (left) of the California Department of Parks and Recreation and Brian O'Neill of the National Parks Service hold up the station's National Historic Landmark plaque. (Photograph by Kenneth Lee; Angel Island Immigration Station Foundation Collection.)

The Angel Island Immigration Station Foundation celebrated the National Historic Landmarks designation on May 16, 1998. The foundation's board of directors and officers at that time were, from left to right, Jim Bow, Jeff Ow, Felicia Lowe, Katherine Toy, Erika Lee, Ginny Yamate, Jim Burke (of Angel Island State Park), Katharine Yee, and Dan Quan. Winning National Historical Landmark status helps the campaign to restore the immigration station as a museum. (Photograph by Kenneth Lee; Angel Island Immigration Station Foundation Collection.)

The Angel Island Immigration Station Foundation held some "visioning" symposia in 1999 to marshal different perspectives on what a future West Coast immigration museum and educational center at Angel Island should be. Dan Iacofono was one of the consultants contributing ideas for restoring the site and making it a destination for people to learn about the West Coast immigration story. (Angel Island Immigration Station Foundation Collection.)

Under her "Save America's Treasures" initiative when she was first lady, Hillary Rodham Clinton supported efforts to preserve the immigration station, and she attended a November 1999 San Francisco reception for the station's preservation efforts. Pictured here with her are Angel Island Immigration Station Foundation officers and board members, from left to right, Dan Quan, Mim Carlson, Hillary Clinton, Katharine Yee, Felicia Lowe (board president), Ginny Yamate, Jeff Ow, Bob Uyeki, and Kathy Ko. (Angel Island Immigration Station Foundation Collection.)

The Angel Island Immigration Station Foundation also has educational programs to tell the story of West Coast immigration history. Pictured here, its "Gateway to Gold Mountain" exhibit, designed by Dan Quan, a San Francisco–born architect and a descendant of Angel Island detainees, has been seen by thousands of people nationwide. Quan has served as foundation president and continues to work on the restoration campaign. (Photograph by Dan Quan.)

Installation artist Flo Oy Wong, left, who created the "made in usa: Angel Island Shhh" exhibition, displayed in the detention barracks in 2000, is with her older sisters, from left to right, Lai Chop Webster, Li Keng Wong, and Nellie Wong. Their parents were detained at the immigration station as were Lai Chop Webster and Li Keng Wong when they were children in 1933. (Photograph by Marvin Collins; Flo Oy Wong collection.)

Five

THE LIGHTHOUSE SERVICE

The very position that made Angel Island a valuable defensive location in foggy San Francisco Bay also made it a hazard to maritime navigation. Ships en route to Mare Island Naval Shipyard in Vallejo and the busy Sacramento River ports all had to pass by the rocky points of Angel Island. After numerous shipwrecks and even more close calls, it was determined that the island needed a lighthouse.

However, instead of a light, a fog bell was installed at Point Knox in 1886. A keeper was hired to keep it ringing, which was chancy at times. The bell operated on a mechanism similar to a giant clock, and it had to be wound up every few hours. When it failed, the keeper had to strike the bell with a hammer, sometimes for as long as 20 hours straight. Besides the Point Knox Lighthouse, one was built at Point Stuart and another was built at Point Blunt in 1915. Eventually, all three had lights as well as bells and foghorns. Of the 14 lighthouses on San Francisco Bay, three were on Angel Island, making it the only island in America with that many.

When built, the Angel Island lighthouses were part of the U.S. Lighthouse Service in the Treasury Department. In 1939, the U.S. Coast Guard absorbed the Lighthouse Service. Only the Point Blunt Lighthouse is still under the jurisdiction of the U.S. Coast Guard and therefore is the only part of Angel Island State Park that is off-limits to visitors.

The residence for the keeper of the Point Knox lighthouse was built on a dramatic, rocky outcropping reachable by a wooden stairway with 151 steps. By 1900, a light had finally been added to the fog-warning equipment. In 1915, a second light was installed at Point Stuart and another keeper was hired. This keeper was also to live at Point Knox. The one-story residence had to be expanded so it was simply raised up and a new floor built underneath. The light and fog bell were in the extension jutting out from the residence. From 1902 until 1914, Juliet Nichols was the keeper of the Point Knox station. She gained fame by striking the fog bell with a hammer for 20 hours when the clockwork failed during heavy fog.

Risky but usable in calm weather, a second set of stairs led down to a water landing. This was needed because transportation of supplies was limited over the primitive roads on Angel Island. The Point Knox lighthouse was closed in 1963 and burned by the U.S. Coast Guard. No trace of the structure remains.

All that was left when the lighthouse burned was the lonely bell that had served on so many foggy days and nights. It now sits on the platform that had been carved out of the cliff for the lighthouse. The 3,000-pound bell may have been too heavy to safely move from its home on the cliff at Point Knox. For whatever reason it remains, it has significant historical importance. Unfortunately, the historical significance of the building was not recognized when it was burned.

The Point Stuart light and fog signal marked the entrance to Raccoon Strait, between Angel Island and the Tiburon shore, which for many years was the main shipping channel. Here it is clear why a residence for the keeper at the one-story building was not built; mountain goats would have to have been hired to service the equipment. The keepers lived at the Point Knox lighthouse.

Although the original structure is still visible from the waterside, the Point Stuart light and fog signal has been replaced by an offshore buoy. As both commercial shipping and recreational boating increased, the main shipping channel was moved to the east side of Angel Island for safety reasons.

In 1915, a light was installed on the end of Point Blunt to assist ships passing on the east side of Angel Island. Because of the proximity of Southampton Shoals, this was a particularly dangerous channel. This light also became the responsibility of the personnel at Point Knox.

When the U.S. Coast Guard abandoned the Point Knox light, all personnel were moved into new quarters at Point Blunt. There were four family units, each with three bedrooms, for the officer in charge and his three assistants. The light was fully automated in 1976. This is the only area of Angel Island that is off-limits to park visitors, although other areas are occasionally restricted for safety reasons.

The automated station still has a green flashing navigation light and a foghorn to use when needed. The prominent location is visible from the entire bay but is especially important since the main shipping channel is now on the east side of Angel Island.

When the Southampton Shoals lighthouse was sold to the St. Francis Yacht Club (and was moved to Tinsley Island in the Delta), its Fresnel lens was saved. Fresnel lenses, used in most coastal and harbor lighthouses, were extremely efficient and could produce a beam that could be seen from 20 miles away. It is now on display at the Visitor Center at the Angel Island State Park headquarters.

Six

NIKE MISSILE BASE

Perhaps the army was a bit hasty in leaving in 1946. The government declared Angel Island surplus to future military needs, closed almost all of the posts, lowered the flag, and moved all army personnel to the Presidio or other bases. The quarantine and immigration stations were already closed, and the island was in the process of being transferred to the Department of the Interior in order to be disposed of to the highest bidder. After all, potential enemies who had the ability to mount a seaborne invasion of the U.S. mainland had been defeated in World War II. But now the Soviet Union, although an ally in that war, had built a fleet of massive bombers based in Siberia that could reach the western United States. And they had the atomic bomb!

Since the San Francisco Bay region would be a primary target in such an attack, schoolchildren rehearsed crouching under their desks, civil defense sirens were tested regularly, and a ring of 12 antiaircraft missile-launching sites were constructed around the bay in 1954. The weapon chosen for this defense was the Nike missile. Based in underground bunkers, the missiles would be raised to the surface and launched to shoot down attacking bombers before they reached the mainland. Guided by a complex system of computers, the Nike-Ajax had a range of 37 miles. The second-generation missile, known as Nike-Hercules, had a range of 87 miles and could be tipped with a nuclear warhead.

The army reoccupied Angel Island in order to construct a Nike missile base. This required removing the top 16 feet of Mount Caroline Livermore to construct a radar control complex and a helicopter-landing pad. A decade later, the army left Angel Island a second time, perhaps for good. The underground bunkers and launching pads remain but are not accessible by visitors.

The Nike system required the coordination of the missile, several radar stations, and computers. Primarily a defensive weapon, the Nike was never used in the United States. After the system was shut down in America, the missiles were shipped overseas to friendly countries that needed protection from enemy aircraft.

Several dozen missiles could be stored in a typical Nike bunker. When an alert was sounded, the crew would move the missiles to an elevator, which brought them to the surface. They were moved by hand to the launch site on wheeled carriages, raised into position, and held in ready for firing.

Nike missile bases were located throughout the Bay Area; the largest installation was on Angel Island. Although army operated, once launched, the main control passed to air force officers at the radar station on the top of Mount Tamalpais. Their long-range radars could look far out to sea and detect enemy bombers long before they reached a release point.

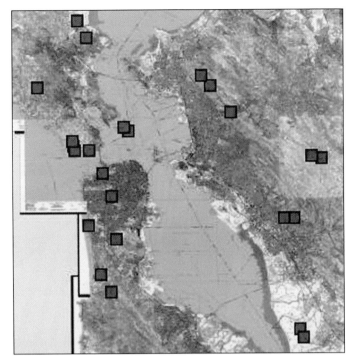

The Nike launch pads (the white streak on the right photograph above) were located near Point Blunt, and launch control was on top of Mount Caroline Livermore (left). After launch, several radar stations tracked the missile while radar on the top of Mount Tamalpais tracked the incoming bombers. Computers used readings from the radars to coordinate the flight of the missile; the Nike-Ajax required a direct hit on an attacking aircraft. Nike Hercules, having an atomic warhead, did not.

To provide a level area for the Nike control and radar equipment on the highest point of Mount Ida (later renamed Mount Caroline Livermore), the top 16 feet were removed. Luckily the dirt was not carted away—just pushed over the side—making it possible to restore the top of the mountain in 2005. A helicopter-landing pad was also constructed. If fired, the missiles would pass right over the control operations, or "over the shoulder" in military parlance.

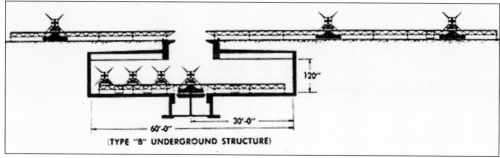

(TYPE "B" UNDERGROUND STRUCTURE)

Underground, reinforced concrete bunkers stored the missiles until called to action. These bunkers are still in place, although most of the surface installations have been removed.

Nike missiles on Angel Island were stored in bombproof, underground bunkers. Crews from U.S. Army D Battery, 9th AA Missile Battalion, who were on duty 24 hours a day, moved the missiles to an elevator, which brought them to the surface.

Once on the surface, the Nike missiles were wheeled into firing position and elevated to await orders from the radar and command stations on top of Angel Island and Mount Tamalpais. That order fortunately never came. By 1962, Inter Continental Ballistic Missiles (ICBMs) had replaced manned bombers in the superpower arsenals, and the Nike missiles became obsolete and were removed from Angel Island. The last Nike missiles in the Bay Area were not taken out of service until 1979.

Once the missiles were removed, the site was abandoned and fenced off from the public. The difficulty and cost of removing such a massive structure made restoring the site impracticable. For historic purposes, a single Nike installation has been left intact at Fort Barry in the Marin headlands. It has missiles but not warheads.

The former hospital at Fort McDowell was converted into headquarters and barracks for the army missile men. Much to the chagrin of those who had served with the medical units at Fort McDowell in the past, the caduceus insignia, or "staff and snakes," over the entrances were covered with the crossed cannons of the field artillery (see page 32).

Seven

THE TRANSITION

In 1939, Hitler invaded Poland and World War II had begun, with the United States maintaining a neutral position but being the "Arsenal of Democracy" to the Allies. The German Afrika Corps and Italian armies in Africa surrendered en masse. Several hundred thousand POWs had to be fed, housed, and guarded, a serious drain on the British. Hundreds of ships bringing food and armaments to the British Isles and returning empty were pressed into service, bringing 363,036 German and a large numbers of Italian POWs to more than 500 camps in America, including Angel Island.

Technically speaking, the Italians on Angel Island were not POWs, as Italy had surrendered before the captured Italians even arrived; however, there was no way to get them home. They were formed into Italian Service Units and sent to work at U.S. military bases. In the Bay Area, they worked in the laundry and kitchens on Angel Island at the Treasure Island Navy Base and elsewhere. While there were some restrictions on their activities during days off, they often headed for North Beach in San Francisco. Inevitably they met local girls and some marriages ensued. A few former Italian soldiers came back after repatriation at the end of the war to live in the Bay Area.

As the immigration and quarantine stations were phased out in the 1930s and 1940s, their properties reverted to the army. On August 18, 1946, the army gave up Angel Island, transferred most of it to the War Assets Administration, who in 1948 gave it to the Department of the Interior for disposal to the highest bidder. However, in 1954, the army reoccupied part of the island to build the Nike missile base, but this only delayed a decision on the fate of the 253 buildings remaining.

In 1957, almost all of the quarantine station was demolished. In 1963, 110 buildings on the island were destroyed without regard to any historical significance. In 1973, even though Angel Island had been placed on the National Register of Historic Places in 1971, almost all of the World War II buildings at Fort Simpton were demolished. Ironically, the Civil War–era buildings at Camp Reynolds, belittled in the army's final inventory as being "beyond economical repair," were spared and are now undergoing restoration.

On August 18, 1946, in a ceremony at Fort McDowell, the remaining troops on the island formed ranks and lowered their flag for the last time. They would return for a decade in the 1950s and 1960s to man the Nike missile battery (see Chapter Six). A century of army occupation of Angel Island would end when they left a second time. It was not a happy day for the men who had served there, but they could be proud of the part they played in recruiting, training, and supporting at least a million soldiers during six wars.

A few soldiers were left behind to "lock up," but by November 1, 1946, the *Salute*, the Angel Island service newspaper printed its last edition. This copy has survived, complete with coffee stains, and is on display at the Fort McDowell chapel.

Tony Brabo, a Marin County contractor, was given the assignment to destroy most of the quarantine station in 1957, and he used an eight-millimeter movie camera to record the work. Many of these images are from his film, and while the quality is not good, it is the only record in existence. The huge tubes used to fumigate baggage and cargo at the quarantine station were rolled down the wharf to a barge, which took them to a scrap yard.

The administration building on the dock, through which all detainees passed before being scrubbed and disinfected, was tough to bring down, but like most of the buildings, it soon would become kindling. The dock was left in place; tour boats and ferries use it today.

The wooden buildings had a heavy steel cable wrapped around them and were simply pulled down with a bulldozer. However, some of the buildings, built of the best grade of redwood, were stubborn and would not fall. One of Brabo's scenes shows the cable passing completely through a building, leaving the building standing but just a bit shorter.

Not even the water storage tanks were spared. Once tipped over, they rolled down the hill and were reduced to kindling by the time they reached the bottom.

Many buildings at Fort McDowell were made of concrete, and the decision was made to leave them standing. Because of vandalism and the danger to the public of large vacant buildings, the decision was made to make them unusable. The huge 1,000-man barrack was gutted. The former tennis courts in the foreground are now covered with picnic tables.

It is possible to see right through many of the buildings, which look like abandoned movie sets.

Not only have the doors been removed at the Fort McDowell hospital, but so has anything made of wood, including floors and trim.

Because transients occupied the hospital, making it dangerous for park rangers to inspect, even the stairways were pulled down, leaving an empty shell of what had been a 110-bed facility. This did provide an opportunity to study the building techniques used a century ago.

Officers Row looks good from a distance, and some buildings are still used by park employees. Most of the homes are boarded up, however, and the exteriors have fallen in to disrepair. They have not been gutted like most of the concrete buildings.

The housing on Officers Row does not stand close inspection—the stairs and porches have rotted away, and the interiors are unusable. Restoration is possible, but the funds are not currently available.

The former commanding officer's seven-bedroom home is now used by park employees as a dormitory. Each employee has a bedroom, and they share a communal kitchen and living area.

Eight

A STATE PARK

As soon as the public realized that Angel Island was no longer going to be preserved by the military, the land rush began. The War Assets Administration put a price of $700,000 on the island. A Citizens Committee to Acquire Angel Island formed quickly in San Francisco to buy and develop "their" Holiday Island, as they called it. Their plans called for a minimum of 300,000 visitors a year, with overnight accommodations for 16,000 people in a variety of hotel and convention facilities. This would provide year-round employment for between 500 and 1,000 people, who would also have housing on the island.

To kick off this scheme, they planned an outing on the island for 10,000 people for Sunday, April 24, 1949, complete with marching bands and rides for the kids. However, apparently no one bothered to check exactly where the island was located. Only two percent was in San Francisco; the other 98 percent was in Marin County. This did not stop San Francisco city planners, though. Until 1968, they were still planning a "Coney Island of the West," even though the 1964 incorporation of the Town of Tiburon included Angel Island.

To the highway departments of various state and local governments, the island was a natural anchor for a transbay bridge or bridges. One scheme envisioned four bridges—one each from San Francisco, Sausalito, Tiburon, and East Bay, all converging into a massive interchange on a flattened out Angel Island. Another plan, which went well beyond the dreaming stage, envisioned a bridge from Tiburon through Angel Island to Telegraph Hill in San Francisco.

In the late 1960s, Pres. Richard Nixon pushed a reluctant Congress into passing legislation that converted military lands into parklands. Thus, in 1972, was born the Golden Gate National Recreation Area, long a dream of Republican congressman William Mailliard, a descendant of one of the original Marin County land grantees. The boundary of the GGNRA included Angel Island; however, much of it had already been transferred to the California State Parks department, who retained control. Most of the other former military reservations in the Bay Area remained under federal control.

A Marin County conservationist, Caroline S. Livermore, founder of the Marin Conservation League, famous for leading the effort to save 900 acres of Richardson Bay for a wildlife sanctuary, was also the driving force behind the state's acquisition of a small part of Angel Island in 1954 and the creation of the state park when more land became available in 1958. Sometimes she had to use her own funds as a deposit to hold land up for sale. She formed the Angel Island Foundation in mid-1950, when the custody of most of Angel Island was transferred to the National Park Service. In 1963, activists were successful in getting all of Angel Island for a state park. The highest peak on Angel Island was named Mount Caroline Livermore in her honor.

Contrary to historical precedent, people en route to Angel Island now eagerly line up on the docks in Tiburon. Bicycles, baby carriages, and picnic baskets are part of today's visitor's luggage.

Luggage today also consists of campers' backpacks, and fumigation on arrival and departure is no longer required! (After a day or two camping, it has been suggested that fumigation might not have been such a bad idea after all.)

Many visitors to the park come in their own boats, but the most popular way is by the Angel Island Ferry from Tiburon, run by the McDonogh family since 1959. It only takes about 20 minutes, and bicycles and camping gear are welcome. Whole scout troops assemble on the Main Street dock and file aboard. Classes, under the watchful eyes of teachers, prepare to spend a day touring the historic exhibits on the island.

The Blue and Gold Fleet of San Francisco Bay commuter boats serve Angel Island from San Francisco during the summer months. Other cruise boats stop by with special parties from time to time. Other carriers bring passengers from East Bay cities and Vallejo on special days.

California State Parks operate this ferry, the *Ayala*, for their employees as many park rangers, staff, gardeners, and maintenance workers live on the island with their families. Others commute from homes on the mainland. If school-age children are part of the families, a special trip is made in the morning and again in the afternoon to accommodate school schedules.

Every navy needs landing craft, and the Angel Island Navy is no exception. The state operates a landing craft to move vehicles to the mainland when they need service. Recycling trucks are brought to the island and returned to the mainland when full, and construction equipment, fire fighting units, and supplies of all kinds are transported on the *Clam*.

When the park first opened to the public the only concession granted was for the Tiburon–Angel Island ferry service. A tractor-drawn trailer was the best available transportation on the island. Hopefully visitors had their sunscreen! (Courtesy of the McDonogh family library.)

Visitors to the park these days can ride a comfortable, articulated "elephant train" to tour the island without walking the difficult trails. The modern tram circles the island, making stops at important and historic sites. It takes about one hour to make the complete circuit.

School groups, Boy Scouts, and Girl Scouts take the history tour and learn about life on the island at the time of the Civil War. The former quartermaster's warehouse has been restored and provides shelter for those who do not bring tents. They even get Civil War–era army caps to wear.

The interior of the warehouse has been remodeled to include sleeping platforms, an old-fashioned kitchen, and a dining area.

Mock bombardments of unseen invaders are conducted as part of Civil War Days events. Docents train regularly, and crowds of picnickers gather to watch. The cannon, smooth-bore muzzle loaders, date back to the early days but are not the ones used to defend against invading fleets of British or Confederate warships that never came.

Docents love to dress up in Civil War–era clothes and entertain visitors with tales of life on the frontier. Some even bake goodies in the restored Bake House, morsels that they will share with visitors.

The love some people have for Angel Island was exemplified by Bob and Mary Noyes. Dr. Noyes and his wife offered to restore Quarters No. 10 at the head of Officers Row at Camp Reynolds, one of the oldest buildings on the island. They first moved into a tent on the grounds and later moved into Quarters No. 10 when the restoration had proceeded to the point that the building was habitable. They raised $500,000 toward the restoration, including a fund for future maintenance. It took three years, but the result was a historically accurate 19th-century officers' quarters, which visitors can tour when docents are present. Volunteer master gardeners come over from the mainland weekly to maintain the grounds of Quarters No. 10 and the adjoining Bake House.

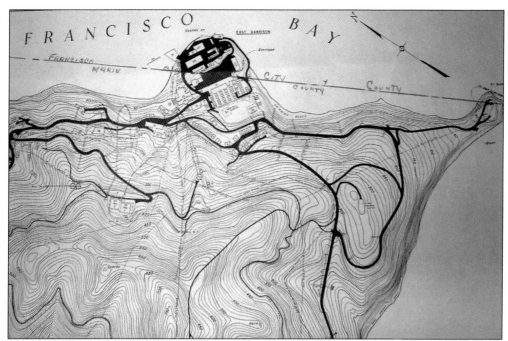

This map of the Fort McDowell area indicates the division between the city of San Francisco and the town of Tiburon. San Francisco, at one time, wanted the state to make this the primary entrance to the park. An elaborate reception area was envisioned but never constructed. Fancy restrooms did get built, however, allowing docents to tease visitors to Fort McDowell by telling them that the nearest restrooms are in San Francisco.

An elaborate new pier, a reception kiosk, and a visitor center were all built on San Francisco's two acres, which also provided access to a restaurant, gift shop, and bicycle rentals. For a variety of reasons, this entrance to the park never opened, and Ayala Cove on the Marin side is still the main access to the island.

The most popular picnicking spot is Ayala Cove. Through the 1960s and 1970s, the Town of Tiburon held an annual outing called Ayala Day, commemorating the early explorer. Seven former mayors celebrating Ayala Day on Angel Island gathered for this photograph. Pictured from left to right are Al Aramburu, Hal Edelstein, Larry Smith, Joan Bergsund, Branwell Fanning, George Ellman (who created Ayala Day), and Phil Bass. Ayala Day often featured a softball game between Tiburon and Belvedere.

It's not the English Channel, but Raccoon Strait is still a challenge for 800 swimmers willing to try to win the Tiburon Mile, an annual race from Ayala Cove to the Corinthian Yacht Club on Main Street in Tiburon.

This attractive building was the administration office of the quarantine station and used for employee housing. Surrounded by picnic tables and barbeques, it is now the headquarters of the park administration and the Angel Island Association. It also houses the Visitor Center on the ground floor with a number of exhibits and park rangers and docents to answer questions.

Angel Island is full of contradictions. It was discovered by a Spanish sea captain who apparently never set foot on the island. It was a fortress from which a shot was never fired in anger. It was an immigration station whose main function was to keep immigrants from entering the country. It held German civilian seamen prisoners while America was not at war with Germany. It was a missile base that never fired a missile. It never had a court, but an important trial was held there. It was the first U.S. port of call for trans-Pacific passenger ships but did not appear on ship's itineraries. Hopefully, this book has made some sense out all of this.